tagines
& couscous

THE AUSTRALIAN
Women's Weekly

contents

North Africa has one of the world's most diverse cultures and this is reflected in its cuisine. Its wide and delicious range of ingredients are showcased in the region's favourite dish – tagines. Tender, slow-cooked aromatic vegetables, and meat that falls off the bone are served alongside couscous or rice. North Africans believe their best food is found in the home – and this book proves it.

Pamela Clark

Food Director

to start

moroccan chicken & chickpea soup

2 tablespoons olive oil
340g chicken breast fillets
1 large brown onion (200g),
  chopped finely
2 cloves garlic, crushed
4 cm piece fresh ginger (20g),
  grated
1½ teaspoons ground cumin
1½ teaspoons ground coriander
1 teaspoon ground turmeric
½ teaspoon sweet paprika

1 cinnamon stick
¼ cup (35g) plain flour
1 litre (4 cups) chicken stock
1 litre (4 cups) water
2 x 300g cans chickpeas, rinsed,
  drained
2 x 400g cans crushed tomatoes
2 tablespoons finely chopped
  preserved lemon
1 tablespoon coarsely chopped
  fresh coriander

1 Heat half the oil in large frying pan; cook chicken, uncovered, about 10 minutes or until browned and cooked through. Drain chicken on absorbent paper, cool 10 minutes; using two forks, shred chicken coarsely.
2 Heat remaining oil in large saucepan; cook onion, garlic and ginger, stirring, until onion softens. Add cumin, ground coriander, turmeric, paprika and cinnamon; cook, stirring, until fragrant.
3 Add flour; cook, stirring, until mixture bubbles and thickens. Gradually stir in stock and the water; cook, stirring, until mixture comes to a boil. Simmer, uncovered, 20 minutes.
4 Add chickpeas and undrained tomatoes, bring to a boil. Reduce heat: simmer, uncovered, 10 minutes.
5 Add chicken and lemon to soup; stir over heat until soup is hot. Just before serving, stir in fresh coriander.

serves 6
prep + cook time 1 hour 10 minutes
per serving 11.3g fat; 1205kJ (288 cal)

harira

··

½ cup (100g) dried chickpeas
500g boned lamb shoulder
2 tablespoons olive oil
1 large brown onion (200g),
    chopped coarsely
2 teaspoons ground ginger
1 tablespoon ground cumin
1 teaspoon ground cinnamon
2 teaspoons ground coriander

6 saffron threads
3 trimmed celery stalks (300g),
    chopped coarsely
7 medium tomatoes (1kg), seeded,
    chopped coarsely
2.5 litres (10 cups) water
½ cup (100g) brown lentils
¼ cup coarsely chopped fresh
    coriander

1 Place chickpeas in small bowl, cover with water; stand overnight, drain.

2 Trim lamb of excess fat; cut into 2cm cubes.

3 Heat oil in large saucepan; cook onion, stirring, until soft. Add spices; cook, stirring, about 2 minutes or until fragrant. Add lamb and celery; cook, stirring, about 2 minutes or until lamb is coated in spice mixture. Add tomato; cook, stirring, about 10 minutes or until tomato softens slightly. Stir in the water and drained chickpeas; bring to a boil. Reduce heat; simmer, covered, about 1½ hours or until lamb is tender, stirring occasionally.

4 Stir in lentils; cook, covered, about 30 minutes or until lentils are just tender.

5 Just before serving, stir coriander into soup.

··

serves 6
prep + cook time 2 hours 30 minutes (plus standing time)
per serving 15.6g fat; 1317kJ (314 cal)
tips Drained canned chickpeas can be substituted for dried chickpeas. Two 400g cans of crushed tomatoes can be substituted for fresh tomatoes.
serving suggestion Serve with lemon wedges and toasted pide.

smoky eggplant caviar

makes 2 cups
prep + cook time 45 minutes
per tablespoon 2.4g fat; 113kJ
(27 cal)

2 large eggplants (1kg)
⅓ cup (80ml) lemon juice
¼ cup (60ml) olive oil
1 clove garlic, crushed

1 Pierce eggplants all over with skewer or sharp knife. Cook on heated oiled grill plate (or grill or barbecue) about 30 minutes or until eggplant softens, turning every 10 minutes. Cool.
2 Halve eggplants, scoop flesh out of skin into fine strainer; discard skin. Drain 5 minutes.
3 Blend or process eggplant until pulpy; transfer to serving bowl. Stir in remaining ingredients.
4 Serve cold or at room temperature, with grissini, if desired.

capsicum dip

4 large red capsicums (1.4kg)
3 cloves garlic, unpeeled
2 tablespoons olive oil
1 tablespoon red wine vinegar
1 tablespoon lemon juice
1 tablespoon finely chopped
   preserved lemon rind
½ teaspoon hot paprika
2 tablespoons finely chopped fresh
   coriander

makes 1½ cups
prep + cook time 45 minutes
per tablespoon 2.2g fat; 155kJ (37 cal)
tip Serve dip with crusty bread; we used
toasted pitta bread.

1 Preheat oven to 220°C/180°C
fan-forced. Oil oven trays.
2 Quarter capsicums; discard seeds
and membranes. Roast, skin-side up,
with garlic about 30 minutes or until
skin blisters and blackens. Cover
capsicum and garlic with plastic
or paper for 5 minutes, then peel
away skins.
3 Blend or process capsicum, garlic,
oil, vinegar, juice, preserved lemon
and paprika until smooth. Stir in
coriander; season to taste.

lamb

pitta salad rolls
with lamb kebabs

500g diced lamb
¼ cup (60ml) lemon juice
1 clove garlic, crushed
⅓ cup (80ml) olive oil
8 pitta pocket breads
80g baby spinach leaves
2 medium tomatoes (300g), sliced thickly
½ cup (60g) seeded black olives, quartered
200g fetta cheese, crumbled

1 Combine lamb, juice, garlic and 2 tablespoons of the oil in large bowl. Cover; refrigerate 3 hours or overnight. Remove lamb from marinade; reserve marinade.
2 Thread lamb onto eight skewers. Heat reserved marinade and remaining oil in large frying pan; cook kebabs, turning, until lamb is cooked as desired.
3 Serve kebabs on pitta bread accompanied with spinach, tomato, olives and cheese.

serves 4
prep + cook time 35 minutes (+ refrigeration time)
per serving 39.5g fat; 3140kJ (750 cal)
tip You need to soak eight bamboo skewers in water for at least an hour before using to stop them from splintering and scorching during cooking.

moroccan lamb shanks with polenta & white beans

1½ cups (300g) dried haricot beans
12 french-trimmed lamb shanks (3kg)
¼ cup (35g) plain flour
1 tablespoon olive oil
2 medium red onions (340g), chopped finely
2 cloves garlic, crushed
2 teaspoons ground cumin
½ teaspoon ground cardamom
½ teaspoon ground ginger
2 teaspoons finely grated lemon rind

⅓ cup (80ml) lemon juice
2 x 400g cans crushed tomatoes
2½ cups (625ml) beef stock
¼ cup (70g) tomato paste
3 cups (750ml) water
3 cups (750ml) milk
2 cups (340g) polenta
2 teaspoons finely grated lemon rind, extra
¼ cup finely chopped fresh flat-leaf parsley
¼ cup finely chopped fresh coriander

1 Cover beans with cold water in large bowl. Stand overnight; drain.

2 Coat lamb in flour; shake off excess. Heat oil in large saucepan; cook lamb, in batches, until browned all over. Add onion and garlic; cook, stirring, until onion is soft. Add spices to pan; cook, stirring, about 2 minutes or until fragrant.

3 Stir in beans, rind, juice, undrained tomatoes, stock and paste; bring to a boil. Reduce heat; simmer, covered, 40 minutes. Uncover; simmer about 50 minutes or until lamb and beans are tender.

4 Heat the water and milk in large saucepan (do not boil). Add polenta; cook, stirring, about 5 minutes or until liquid is absorbed and polenta softens.

5 Serve lamb mixture on polenta; sprinkle with combined extra rind, parsley and coriander.

serves 6
prep + cook time 2 hours 25 minutes (+ standing time)
per serving 15.1g fat; 3114kJ (744 cal)
tip You can use any dried bean (navy, cannellini, great northern or even chickpeas) in this recipe.

lamb & vegetable stew

serves 8
prep + cook time 2 hours 20 minutes
per serving 18.4g fat; 2253kJ
(538 cal)
tip Use fresh broad beans, if in
season.

2 tablespoons olive oil
2 medium red onions (340g),
  chopped coarsely
1½ teaspoons ground ginger
½ teaspoon ground cinnamon
2 x 400g cans crushed tomatoes
1.5 litres (6 cups) vegetable stock
pinch saffron threads
1kg diced lamb
1 cup (200g) white long-grain rice
1 cup (200g) red lentils
2 x 400g cans chickpeas, rinsed,
  drained
1kg frozen broad beans, thawed,
  peeled
½ cup coarsely chopped fresh
  coriander leaves
½ cup coarsely chopped fresh
  flat-leaf parsley

1 Heat oil in large heavy-based
saucepan; cook onion, ginger and
cinnamon, stirring, until onion is soft.
2 Add undrained tomatoes, stock,
saffron and lamb; bring to a boil.
Simmer, covered, about 1½ hours or
until lamb is tender.
3 Add rice and lentils; simmer,
uncovered, about 20 minutes or until
rice and lentils are just tender. Add
chickpeas and beans; simmer,
uncovered, until hot. Just before
serving, stir through coriander and
parsley.

lamb hot pot with couscous

600g lamb leg chops
1 tablespoon plain flour
2 teaspoons olive oil
1 medium brown onion (150g),
    cut into thin wedges
1 teaspoon ground cinnamon
1 teaspoon ground turmeric
1 cup water (250ml)
½ cup beef stock (125ml)
100g prunes, seeded
2 tablespoons finely chopped
    fresh coriander

couscous
1 cup (250ml) boiling water
1 cup (200g) couscous

serves 2
prep + cook time 1 hour
per serving 20.3g fat; 3648kJ
(871 cal)

1 Trim all visible fat from lamb. Cut
lamb into cubes; toss in flour.
2 Heat oil in large saucepan; cook
onion until soft. Add lamb; cook until
browned all over. Stir in cinnamon
and turmeric; cook 1 minute.
3 Stir in the water, stock and prunes;
bring to a boil. Reduce heat; simmer,
covered, about 30 minutes or until
lamb is tender.
4 Meanwhile, make couscous.
5 Serve lamb with couscous;
sprinkle with coriander.

couscous Combine the water and
couscous in medium bowl; stand
5 minutes or until liquid is absorbed,
fluffing with fork occasionally.

kofta with fresh green onion couscous

1kg minced lamb
1 medium brown onion (150g), chopped finely
2 cloves garlic, crushed
2 tablespoons lemon juice
1½ teaspoons ground cumin
1½ teaspoons ground coriander
¼ cup (40g) roasted pine nuts
2 tablespoons finely chopped fresh mint
1 tablespoon finely chopped fresh coriander
1 egg
2 cups (500ml) beef stock
2 cups (400g) couscous
30g butter, chopped
2 green onions, sliced thinly

1 Combine mince, brown onion, garlic, juice, spices, nuts, herbs and egg in large bowl. Roll heaped tablespoons of mixture into balls; thread three balls on each skewer. Place kofta skewers on tray, cover; refrigerate 30 minutes.

2 Place stock in medium saucepan; bring to a boil. Remove from heat, add couscous and butter, cover; stand about 5 minutes or until liquid is absorbed, fluffing with fork occasionally.

3 Meanwhile, cook kofta on heated oiled grill plate (or grill or barbecue) until browned all over and cooked through.

4 Toss green onion with couscous; serve with kofta, accompanied by a bowl of combined yogurt and chopped cucumber, if desired.

serves 4
prep + cook time 35 minutes (+ refrigeration time)
per serving 42.7g fat; 4114kJ (983 cal)
tip Soak 12 bamboo skewers in cold water for at least 1 hour before use to prevent scorching and splintering.

lamb tagine with ras el hanout

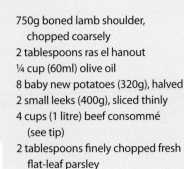

serves 4
prep + cook time 1 hour
(+ refrigeration time)
per serving 25.7g fat; 2023kJ (484 cal)
tip Use either canned or packaged consommé for a good flavour, but if you prefer, use stock instead.

750g boned lamb shoulder, chopped coarsely
2 tablespoons ras el hanout
¼ cup (60ml) olive oil
8 baby new potatoes (320g), halved
2 small leeks (400g), sliced thinly
4 cups (1 litre) beef consommé (see tip)
2 tablespoons finely chopped fresh flat-leaf parsley

1 Combine lamb, ras el hanout and 1 tablespoon of the oil in large bowl. Cover, refrigerate 3 hours or overnight.
2 Preheat oven to 200°C/180°C fan-forced.
3 Heat 1 tablespoon of the remaining oil in tagine or flameproof casserole dish on stove top; cook lamb, in batches, until browned. Remove from tagine.
4 Heat remaining oil in same tagine; cook potato and leek, stirring, until potatoes are browned lightly and leek softens. Return lamb to tagine with consommé; bring to the boil.
5 Cover tagine, transfer to oven; cook about 45 minutes or until lamb is tender. Remove from oven; stir in parsley. Season to taste.

moroccan lamb with couscous

8 lamb fillets (800g)
1 tablespoon ground cumin
1 tablespoon ground coriander
1 teaspoon ground cinnamon
¾ cup (210g) low-fat yogurt
1½ cups (300g) couscous
1½ cups (375ml) boiling water
1 teaspoon peanut oil
⅓ cup (55g) dried currants
2 teaspoons finely grated lemon
   rind
2 teaspoons lemon juice
¼ cup coarsely chopped fresh
   coriander leaves

serves 4
prep + cook time 30 minutes
(+ refrigeration time)
per serving 9.3g fat; 2193kJ (524 cal)
tip Substitute some finely chopped
preserved lemon for the lemon juice
and rind in the couscous.

1 Combine lamb, spices and ⅓ cup
of the yogurt in medium bowl, cover;
refrigerate 3 hours or overnight.
2 Cook lamb on heated oiled grill
plate (or grill or barbecue) until
browned and cooked as desired.
Cover; stand 5 minutes then slice
thinly.
3 Meanwhile, combine couscous,
the water and oil in large heatproof
bowl, cover; stand 5 minutes or until
liquid is absorbed, fluffing with fork
occasionally. Stir in currants, rind,
juice and fresh coriander; toss with
fork to combine.
4 Serve lamb with couscous; drizzle
with remaining yogurt.

lamb & apricot tagine with orange & lemon couscous

1⅔ cups (250g) dried apricots
¾ cup (180ml) orange juice
½ cup (125ml) boiling water
2 tablespoons olive oil
900g diced lamb
2 medium red capsicums (400g), chopped coarsely
1 large brown onion (200g), chopped coarsely
2 medium kumara (800g), chopped coarsely
3 cloves garlic, crushed
1 teaspoon ground cinnamon
2 teaspoons ground cumin

2 teaspoons ground coriander
1 cup (250ml) dry red wine
1 litre (4 cups) chicken stock
2 tablespoons honey
1 cup loosely packed fresh coriander leaves
¾ cup (200g) low-fat yogurt

orange & lemon couscous
1 litre (4 cups) water
4 cups (800g) couscous
1 tablespoon finely grated orange rind
2 teaspoons finely grated lemon rind
2 teaspoons finely grated lime rind

1 Combine apricots, juice and the water in small bowl. Cover; stand 45 minutes.
2 Meanwhile, heat half the oil in large saucepan; cook lamb, in batches, until browned all over.
3 Heat remaining oil in same pan; cook capsicum, onion, kumara, garlic and ground spices, stirring, until onion softens and mixture is fragrant. Add wine, bring to a boil; simmer, uncovered, about 5 minutes or until liquid reduces by half.
4 Return lamb to pan with undrained apricots, stock and honey; bring to a boil. Reduce heat, simmer, covered, about 50 minutes or until lamb is tender. Remove from heat; stir in fresh coriander. Make orange and lemon couscous.
5 Serve lamb and apricot tagine on couscous; drizzle with yogurt.

orange and lemon couscous Bring the water to a boil in medium saucepan; stir in couscous and rinds. Remove from heat; stand, covered, about 5 minutes or until liquid is absorbed, fluffing with fork occasionally.

serves 8
prep + cook time 1 hour 20 minutes (+ standing time)
per serving 12.8g fat;1837kJ (439 cal)

beef & veal

veal cutlets with couscous salad

8 veal cutlets (1.5kg)
⅓ cup (80ml) balsamic vinegar
⅓ cup (80ml) olive oil
1 clove garlic, crushed
1½ cups (375ml) beef stock
1½ cups (300g) couscous
150g fetta cheese, cut into 2cm pieces
⅔ cup (120g) seeded kalamata olives
1 medium red capsicum (200g), chopped coarsely
¼ cup coarsely chopped fresh mint
¼ cup (60ml) lemon juice
⅓ cup (80ml) olive oil, extra
1 clove garlic, crushed

1 Combine cutlets in large bowl with vinegar, oil and garlic; toss to coat cutlets all over in marinade. Cover; refrigerate 20 minutes.
2 Meanwhile, bring stock to a boil in medium saucepan. Remove from heat; stir in couscous. Cover; stand about 5 minutes or until liquid is absorbed, fluffing with fork occasionally. Add remaining ingredients; toss gently to combine.
3 Drain cutlets; discard marinade. Cook cutlets on heated oiled grill plate (or grill or barbecue) until browned both sides and cooked as desired. Serve couscous salad with cutlets.

serves 4
prep + cook time 20 minutes (+ refrigeration time)
per serving 50.8g fat; 4094kJ (978 cal)

moroccan beef with citrus couscous

2 cloves garlic, crushed
1 teaspoon ground ginger
1 tablespoon ground cumin
2 teaspoons ground coriander
500g piece beef butt fillet
1 tablespoon harissa paste
1 cup (250ml) beef stock
200g seeded green olives, crushed
  lightly
½ cup coarsely chopped fresh
  coriander

citrus couscous
2 medium oranges (480g)
1 cup (250ml) water
1 cup (250ml) orange juice
2 cups (400g) couscous
¼ cup (35g) roasted slivered almonds
1 tablespoon thinly sliced preserved
  lemon
1 small red onion (100g), sliced thinly
500g red radishes, trimmed,
  sliced thinly

1 Combine garlic and spices in medium bowl; reserve about a third of the spice mixture. Add beef to bowl with remaining spice mixture; toss to coat beef all over. Cook beef on heated oiled grill plate (or grill or barbecue) until charred lightly both sides and cooked as desired. Cover; stand 10 minutes then slice thickly.

2 Meanwhile, make citrus couscous.

3 Cook harissa and remaining spice mixture in dry heated small frying pan until fragrant. Add stock; bring to a boil. Reduce heat; simmer, uncovered, about 3 minutes or until harissa dressing reduces by half. Remove from heat; stir in olives and coriander.

4 Serve beef on citrus couscous; drizzle with warm harissa dressing.

citrus couscous Remove skin and white pith from oranges; cut in half, slice thinly. Place the water and juice in medium saucepan; bring to a boil. Remove from heat; stir in couscous. Cover; stand about 5 minutes or until liquid is absorbed, fluffing with fork occasionally. Add orange and remaining ingredients; toss gently to combine.

serves 4
prep + cook time 35 minutes
per serving 15.5g fat; 3114kJ (744 cal)
tip Butt fillet is fillet from the rump; rump steak can be substituted, if preferred.

meatball tagine with eggs

500g minced beef
1 clove garlic, crushed
¼ cup finely chopped fresh mint
2 tablespoons finely chopped fresh coriander
1 teaspoon ground cinnamon
1 teaspoon ground coriander
2 teaspoons ground cumin
½ teaspoon chilli powder
1 tablespoon olive oil
1 medium brown onion (150g), chopped finely
4 large tomatoes (880g), chopped coarsely
pinch saffron threads
4 eggs
½ cup loosely packed fresh coriander leaves

1 Combine mince, garlic, mint, chopped coriander, cinnamon, ground coriander, half the cumin and half the chilli in large bowl; season. Roll level tablespoons of mixture into balls.

2 Heat oil in tagine or large frying pan; cook meatballs, in batches, until browned. Remove from tagine.

3 Stir onion in same heated tagine until softened. Add tomato, saffron and remaining cumin and chilli; bring to the boil. Simmer, uncovered, about 15 minutes or until tomatoes soften.

4 Return meatballs to pan; simmer, uncovered, about 10 minutes or until meatballs are cooked and sauce thickens slightly. Season to taste. Carefully crack eggs into tagine; simmer, covered, about 5 minutes or until eggs are barely set. Sprinkle tagine with coriander leaves.

serves 4
prep + cook time 1 hour
per serving 20.2g fat; 1488kJ (356 cal)
tip Serve with crusty bread.

beef, raisin & almond tagine

serves 4
prep + cook time 1 hour 30 minutes
per serving 22.1g fat; 1630kJ
(390 cal)

1 tablespoon olive oil
625g beef chuck steak, chopped
  coarsely
1 medium brown onion (150g),
  chopped coarsely
2 cloves garlic, crushed
2 teaspoons ras el hanout
½ teaspoon ground ginger
½ teaspoon ground cinnamon
1 dried bay leaf
1 cup (250ml) beef stock
¼ cup (35g) coarsely chopped
  raisins
¼ cup (40g) blanched almonds,
  roasted

1 Heat oil in tagine or large frying
pan; cook beef, in batches, until
browned. Remove from tagine.
2 Stir onion in same heated tagine
until softened. Add garlic, spices and
bay leaf; cook, stirring, until fragrant.
Return beef to pan with stock; bring
to the boil. Reduce heat; simmer,
covered, 1 hour. Add raisins; simmer,
uncovered, about 15 minutes or until
beef is tender and tagine thickens.
Stir in nuts, season to taste;
accompany with lemon wedges.

beef & eggplant tagine

2 tablespoons olive oil
625g beef chuck steak, chopped
   coarsely
1 medium brown onion (150g),
   chopped coarsely
2 cloves garlic, crushed
2 teaspoons ground coriander
1 teaspoon ground ginger
1 teaspoon ground cumin
1 teaspoon sweet paprika
½ cup (125ml) beef stock
3 medium tomatoes (450g),
   chopped coarsely
3 baby eggplants (180g), sliced
   thickly

serves 4
prep + cook time 1 hour 30 minutes
per serving 21.2g fat; 1538kJ
(368 cal)

1 Heat half the oil in tagine or large saucepan; cook beef, in batches, until browned. Remove from tagine.

2 Stir onion in same heated tagine until softened. Add garlic and spices; cook, stirring, until fragrant. Return beef to tagine with stock and tomato; bring to the boil. Reduce heat; simmer, covered, 45 minutes. Uncover; simmer about 30 minutes or until beef is tender and tagine thickens.

3 Meanwhile, heat remaining oil in medium frying pan; cook eggplant, stirring, about 10 minutes or until browned and tender. Stir eggplant into tagine; season to taste.

beef & prune tagine
with spinach couscous

....

2 large red onions (600g), chopped
   finely
2 tablespoons olive oil
1 teaspoon cracked black pepper
pinch saffron threads
1 teaspoon ground cinnamon
¼ teaspoon ground ginger
1kg beef blade steak, diced into
   4cm pieces
50g butter, chopped
425g can diced tomatoes

1 cup (250ml) water
2 tablespoons white sugar
¾ cup (100g) roasted slivered almonds
1½ cups (250g) seeded prunes
1 teaspoon finely grated lemon rind
¼ teaspoon ground cinnamon, extra

spinach couscous
1½ cups (300g) couscous
1½ cups (375ml) boiling water
80g finely shredded baby spinach leaves

1 Combine onion, oil and spices in large bowl, add beef; toss beef to coat
in mixture.
2 Place beef in large deep saucepan with butter, undrained tomatoes, the water,
half the sugar and ½ cup of the nuts; bring to a boil. Simmer, covered, 1½ hours.
Remove 1 cup cooking liquid; reserve. Simmer tagine, uncovered, 30 minutes.
3 Meanwhile, place prunes in small bowl, cover with boiling water; stand
20 minutes, drain. Place prunes in small saucepan with rind, extra cinnamon,
remaining sugar and reserved cooking liquid; bring to a boil. Reduce heat; simmer,
uncovered, about 15 minutes or until prunes soften. Stir into tagine.
4 Make spinach couscous.
5 Divide couscous and tagine among serving plates; sprinkle tagine with
remaining nuts.

spinach couscous Combine couscous and the water in large heatproof bowl,
cover; stand about 5 minutes or until water is absorbed, fluffing with fork
occasionally. Stir in spinach.

....

serves 4
prep + cook time 2 hours 50 minutes
per serving 50.3g fat; 4799kJ (1148 cal)

fish & chicken

moroccan blue-eye fillets with fruity couscous

1 clove garlic, crushed
1cm piece fresh ginger (5g), grated
1 teaspoon ground cumin
½ teaspoon ground turmeric
½ teaspoon hot paprika
½ teaspoon ground coriander
4 x 200g blue-eye fillets, skin removed
1 tablespoon olive oil

fruity couscous
2 cups (400g) couscous
2 cups (500ml) boiling water
50g butter
1 large pear (330g), chopped finely
½ cup (80g) finely chopped dried apricots
½ cup (100g) coarsely chopped dried figs
½ cup coarsely chopped fresh flat-leaf parsley
¼ cup (40g) roasted pine nuts

1 Combine garlic, ginger and spices in large bowl. Add fish; toss to coat fish in spice mixture. Heat oil in large frying pan; cook fish, in batches, until browned both sides and cooked as desired.
2 Meanwhile, make fruity couscous.
3 Divide couscous among serving plates; top with fish. Accompany with a bowl of combined yogurt and coarsely chopped fresh coriander, if desired.

fruity couscous Combine couscous, the water and butter in large heatproof bowl, cover; stand about 5 minutes or until liquid is absorbed, fluffing with fork occasionally. Stir in remaining ingredients.

serves 4
prep + cook time 35 minutes
per serving 27.5g fat; 3816kJ (912 cal)

spicy prawn & tomato tagine

1 tablespoon olive oil
1 medium brown onion (150g), chopped finely
3 cloves garlic, crushed
1 teaspoon ground ginger
1 teaspoon ground cumin
¼ teaspoon chilli powder
pinch saffron threads
1kg tomatoes, chopped coarsely
1.5kg uncooked medium king prawns
¼ cup finely chopped fresh flat-leaf parsley
¼ cup finely chopped fresh coriander
¼ cup (30g) finely chopped roasted unsalted pistachios
1 tablespoon finely chopped preserved lemon rind

1   Heat oil in tagine or flameproof casserole dish; cook onion and garlic, stirring, until onion softens. Add spices; cook, stirring, about 1 minute or until fragrant. Add tomato; cook, stirring, about 5 minutes or until tomato softens. Bring to the boil. Reduce heat; simmer, stirring occasionally, about 10 minutes or until sauce thickens slightly.
2   Meanwhile, shell and devein prawns leaving tails intact. Add prawns to pan; cook, covered, stirring occasionally, about 5 minutes or until prawns are changed in colour. Season to taste.
3   Combine herbs, nuts and preserved lemon in small bowl.
4   Serve tagine sprinkled with herb mixture.

serves 6
prep + cook time 40 minutes
per serving 6.6g fat; 857kJ (205 cal)
tip Serve with couscous or crusty bread.

chilli fish tagine

serves 4
prep + cook time 30 minutes
(+ refrigeration time)
per serving 21.1g fat; 1956kJ (468 cal)
tip Mustard seed oil can be found in health-food shops, delis and some supermarkets. If you prefer, use olive oil.

4 x 200g white fish fillets, skin on
1 tablespoon finely grated lemon rind
2 teaspoons dried chilli flakes
2 cloves garlic, crushed
1 tablespoon mustard seed oil
30g butter
2 baby fennel bulbs (260g), trimmed, cut into wedges
150g green beans, halved lengthways
⅓ cup (50g) raisins
1 cup (250ml) dry white wine
pinch saffron threads
⅓ cup (45g) roasted unsalted pistachios

1 Combine fish, rind, chilli, garlic and oil in large mixing bowl; cover, refrigerate 3 hours or overnight.
2 Melt butter in tagine or large frying pan; cook fennel, stirring, until browned lightly. Add beans, raisins, wine and saffron; top with fish. Bring to the boil. Reduce heat; simmer, covered, about 15 minutes or until fish is cooked as desired. Season to taste.
3 Serve tagine sprinkled with nuts.

chicken, cinnamon & prune tagine

2 tablespoons olive oil
2kg chicken thigh fillets
3 teaspoons cumin seeds
3 teaspoons ground coriander
1 tablespoon smoked paprika
3 teaspoons ground cumin
4 cinnamon sticks
4 medium brown onions (600g),
   sliced thinly
8 cloves garlic, crushed
3 cups (750ml) chicken stock
1 cup (250ml) dry red wine
1 cup (170g) seeded prunes
½ cup (80g) roasted blanched
   almonds
¼ cup coarsely chopped fresh
   flat-leaf parsley

serves 8
prep + cook time 1 hour 50 minutes
per serving 28.8g fat; 2236kJ
(535 cal)

1 Heat half the oil in large saucepan; cook chicken, in batches, until browned.

2 Meanwhile, dry-fry spices in small heated frying pan, stirring, until fragrant.

3 Heat remaining oil in same saucepan; cook onion and garlic, stirring, until onion softens. Return chicken to pan with spices, stock and wine; bring to a boil. Simmer, covered, 40 minutes.

4 Stir in prunes; simmer, uncovered, about 20 minutes or until chicken is tender. Stir in nuts and parsley.

spicy couscous chicken with fresh corn salsa

½ teaspoon ground cumin
¼ teaspoon ground coriander
¼ teaspoon garam masala
¼ teaspoon ground turmeric
1 cup (250ml) chicken stock
1 cup (200g) couscous
700g chicken breast fillets
1 egg white, beaten lightly
2 trimmed corn cobs (500g)
2 medium tomatoes (300g), seeded, chopped coarsely
1 small avocado (200g), chopped coarsely
2 tablespoons red wine vinegar
4 green onions, chopped finely

1 Preheat oven to 220°C/200°C fan-forced.
2 Place spices in medium saucepan; cook, stirring, over medium heat, until fragrant; add stock. Bring to a boil; stir in couscous. Remove from heat; stand, covered, about 5 minutes or until liquid is absorbed, fluffing with fork occasionally.
3 Coat chicken with egg white then with couscous. Place chicken in large lightly oiled baking dish; bake, uncovered, about 10 minutes or until chicken is cooked through. Cover to keep warm.
4 Meanwhile, remove kernels from corn cobs. Cook kernels in small pan of boiling water, uncovered, about 2 minutes or until just tender; drain. Rinse under cold water; drain. Combine corn with remaining ingredients in medium bowl. Serve corn salsa with thickly sliced chicken.

serves 4
prep + cook time 30 minutes
per serving 19.1g fat; 2515kJ (600 cal)

chicken tagine with olives & preserved lemon

....

1 tablespoon olive oil
1 tablespoon butter
8 chicken thigh cutlets (1.5kg), skin removed
1 large red onion (300g), chopped finely
½ teaspoon saffron threads, roasted, crushed
1 teaspoon ground cinnamon
1 teaspoon ground ginger
1½ cups (375ml) chicken stock
16 seeded large green olives
2 tablespoons finely chopped preserved lemon

1   Heat oil and butter in large heavy-based saucepan with tight-fitting lid; cook chicken, in batches, until browned all over.

2   Place onion and spices in same pan; cook, stirring, until onion softens. Return chicken to pan with stock; bring to a boil. Reduce heat; simmer, covered, about 30 minutes or until chicken is cooked through.

3   Remove chicken from pan; cover to keep warm. Skim and discard fat from top of pan liquid; bring to a boil. Reduce heat; cook, stirring, until liquid reduces by half.

4   Return chicken to pan with olives and lemon; stir until heated through. Serve tagine with couscous, if desired.

....

serves 4
prep + cook time 1 hour
per serving 25.9g fat; 1831kJ (437)
tip Saffron threads should be roasted in a small dry frying pan over medium heat until just fragrant, then crushed with the back of a spoon.

spiced apricot & chicken tagine

1 tablespoon olive oil
1kg chicken thigh fillets, chopped coarsely
2 cloves garlic, crushed
1 large brown onion (200g), chopped finely
¼ teaspoon ground cinnamon
½ teaspoon ground cumin
½ teaspoon ground ginger
½ teaspoon ground turmeric
1 cup (250ml) hot chicken stock
1 tablespoon honey
1 cup (150g) dried apricots
1 tablespoon cornflour
1 tablespoon water
½ cup (80g) blanched almonds
2 tablespoons coarsely chopped fresh coriander

1 Combine oil, chicken, garlic, onion and spices in large microwave-safe bowl; cook, covered, on MEDIUM-HIGH (70%) 15 minutes, stirring once during cooking.
2 Add stock, honey and apricots; cook, uncovered, on MEDIUM-HIGH (70%) about 5 minutes or until apricots are tender. Stir in blended cornflour and the water; cook, uncovered, on MEDIUM-HIGH (70%) about 3 minutes or until mixture boils and thickens slightly, stirring once during cooking.
3 Cook nuts on microwave-safe plate, uncovered, on HIGH (100%) about 3 minutes or until browned lightly, stirring twice during cooking. Stir nuts and coriander into tagine; serve with couscous, if desired.

serves 4
prep + cook time 55 minutes
per serving 26.8g fat; 2450kJ (585 cal)

vegetables & couscous

white bean & lentil tagine

1 tablespoon olive oil
1 medium brown onion (150g), chopped coarsely
2 cloves garlic, crushed
2.5cm piece fresh ginger (15g), cut into matchsticks
1 teaspoon harissa
800g canned whole peeled tomatoes, chopped coarsely
1 medium red capsicum (200g), chopped coarsely
½ cup (125ml) water
400g canned cannellini beans, rinsed, drained
400g canned brown lentils, rinsed, drained
¼ cup finely chopped fresh mint
¼ cup finely chopped fresh flat-leaf parsley

1 Heat oil in tagine or large frying pan; stir onion until softened. Add garlic, ginger and paste; cook, stirring, about 1 minute or until fragrant.
2 Add undrained tomatoes, capsicum, the water, beans and lentils; bring to the boil. Reduce heat; simmer, uncovered, about 15 minutes or until tagine thickens. Remove from heat; stir in mint, season to taste.
3 Serve tagine sprinkled with parsley.

serves 4
prep + cook time 40 minutes
per serving 5.8g fat; 865kJ (207 cal)
tip Serve with grilled flatbread.

vegetables with harissa & almond couscous

20g butter
1 tablespoon olive oil
2 medium brown onions (300g), chopped coarsely
2 cloves garlic, crushed
4cm piece fresh ginger (20g), grated
2 teaspoons ground cumin
2 teaspoons ground coriander
2 teaspoons finely grated lemon rind
1kg pumpkin, chopped coarsely
400g can chopped tomatoes
2 cups (500ml) vegetable stock

400g green beans, cut into 5cm lengths
⅓ cup (55g) sultanas
1 tablespoon honey
¼ cup finely chopped fresh flat-leaf parsley
¼ cup finely chopped fresh mint

harissa & almond couscous
2 cups (500ml) vegetable stock
1 cup (250ml) water
3 cups (600g) couscous
½ cup (70g) roasted slivered almonds
1 tablespoon harissa

1 Heat butter and oil in large saucepan; cook onion and garlic, stirring, 5 minutes. Add ginger, spices and rind; cook about 1 minute or until fragrant. Add pumpkin, undrained tomatoes and stock; bring to a boil. Reduce heat; simmer, covered, about 15 minutes or until pumpkin is just tender.

2 Make harissa and almond couscous.

3 Add beans to tagine mixture; cook, stirring, 5 minutes. Stir sultanas, honey and chopped herbs through tagine off the heat just before serving; serve with couscous.

harissa & almond couscous Bring stock and the water to a boil in medium saucepan; remove from heat. Add couscous; cover, stand about 3 minutes or until liquid is absorbed, fluffing with fork occasionally. Use fork to gently mix almonds and harissa through couscous.

serves 6
prep + cook time 1 hour
per serving 14.4g fat; 2668kJ (637 cal)

lemon-fetta couscous with steamed vegetables

serves 4
prep + cook time 30 minutes
per serving 9.4g fat; 2427kJ
(581 cal)

600g butternut pumpkin, chopped
    coarsely
2 small green zucchini (180g),
    chopped coarsely
2 small yellow zucchini (180g),
    chopped coarsely
300g spinach, trimmed, chopped
    coarsely
2 cups (500ml) vegetable stock
2 cups (400g) couscous
¼ cup (60ml) lemon juice
⅓ cup coarsely chopped fresh basil
200g low-fat fetta cheese, chopped
    coarsely
¼ cup finely chopped preserved
    lemon rind
6 green onions, sliced thinly

1 Boil, steam or microwave
pumpkin, zucchinis and spinach,
separately, until tender; drain.
2 Meanwhile, bring stock to a boil in
large saucepan. Add couscous,
remove from heat, cover; stand about
5 minutes or until liquid is absorbed,
fluffing with fork occasionally. Place
couscous and vegetables in large
bowl with remaining ingredients; toss
gently to combine.

roasted vegetable couscous

1 medium red onion (170g),
   cut into wedges
4 small zucchini (360g), halved
   lengthways
10 baby carrots (175g), halved
   lengthways
2 tablespoons olive oil
1 cup (200g) couscous
1 cup (250ml) boiling water
450g bottled roasted red capsicum,
   drained, sliced thinly
2 tablespoons finely chopped
   fresh thyme

serves 6
prep + cook time 35 minutes
per serving 8.3g fat; 995kJ (238 cal)
tips Serve with a dollop of plain
yogurt. To save time, use any leftover
or store-bought roasted vegetables
in this recipe.

1 Preheat oven to 220°C/200°C
fan-forced.
2 Combine onion, zucchini, carrot
and oil in large shallow baking dish;
season. Roast, uncovered, about
20 minutes or until vegetables are
tender.
3 Combine couscous with the
water in large heatproof bowl, cover;
stand about 5 minutes or until liquid
is absorbed, fluffing with fork
occasionally.
4 Stir vegetables and remaining
ingredients into couscous; season
to taste.

vegetable couscous

1 medium kumara (400g)
1 tablespoon olive oil
60g butter
4 baby eggplants (240g), sliced thinly
1 large brown onion (200g), sliced thinly
¼ teaspoon cayenne pepper
2 teaspoons ground cumin
2 teaspoons ground coriander
1½ cups (375ml) vegetable stock
2 cups (400g) couscous
2 teaspoons finely grated lemon rind
2 cups (500ml) boiling water
410g can chickpeas, rinsed, drained
2 tablespoons lemon juice
100g baby spinach leaves
¼ cup loosely packed fresh flat-leaf parsley leaves

1 Chop kumara into 1cm cubes. Heat oil and half the butter in large frying pan; cook kumara with eggplant and onion, stirring, until vegetables brown. Add spices; cook about 2 minutes or until fragrant. Stir in stock; bring to a boil. Reduce heat; simmer, uncovered, about 15 minutes or until vegetables are just tender.
2 Meanwhile, combine couscous in large heatproof bowl with rind, the water and half the remaining butter. Cover; stand about 5 minutes or until liquid is absorbed, fluffing occasionally with fork.
3 Add chickpeas and remaining butter to vegetable mixture; cook, stirring, until butter melts. Stir in couscous, juice, spinach and parsley.

serves 4
prep + cook time 45 minutes
per serving 20.1g fat; 3246kJ (775 cal)
tips Remove vegetable mixture from heat, then immediately add couscous, spinach and parsley; the greens will wilt in the heat of the vegetables.
Serve with a bowl of cumin-scented yogurt and warm fresh pitta.

couscous cakes with mediterranean vegetables

1½ tablespoons olive oil
1 medium red onion (170g), sliced thickly
3 baby eggplant (180g), sliced thickly
2 medium green zucchini (240g), chopped coarsely
250g cherry tomatoes
250g yellow teardrop tomatoes
¼ cup (60ml) balsamic vinegar
1 clove garlic, crushed
1½ cups (300g) couscous
1½ cups (375ml) boiling water
¼ cup (20g) finely grated parmesan cheese
2 tablespoons coarsely chopped fresh basil
60g butter

1 Heat 2 teaspoons of the oil in large frying pan; cook onion, eggplant and zucchini, stirring, until vegetables soften.
2 Stir in tomatoes, vinegar, garlic and remaining oil; cook, stirring occasionally, about 10 minutes or until tomatoes are very soft.
3 Meanwhile, combine couscous with the water in large heatproof bowl; cover, stand 5 minutes or until liquid is absorbed, fluffing with fork occasionally. Stir in cheese and basil.
4 Heat half the butter in large frying pan, press half the couscous mixture into four egg rings in pan; cook until browned lightly on both sides. Carefully remove egg rings, then couscous cakes. Repeat using remaining butter and couscous mixture.
5 Serve vegetables with couscous cakes.

serves 4
prep + cook time 35 minutes
per serving 21.7g fat; 2153kJ (514 cal)

preserved lemon & olive couscous

serves 6
prep time 15 minutes
per serving 5.3g fat; 1020kJ
(244 cal)

1¼ cups (250g) couscous
1¼ cups (310ml) boiling water
15g butter
400g canned chickpeas, rinsed,
    drained
½ cup (60g) seeded green olives,
    chopped coarsely
2 tablespoons lemon juice
3 green onions, sliced thinly
2 tablespoons finely chopped fresh
    flat-leaf parsley
1 tablespoon thinly sliced preserved
    lemon rind

1 Combine couscous with the water
and butter in large heatproof bowl,
cover; stand about 5 minutes or until
water is absorbed, fluffing with fork
occasionally.
2 Stir remaining ingredients into
couscous; season to taste.

spicy roasted pumpkin couscous

1 tablespoon olive oil
2 cloves garlic, crushed
1 large red onion (300g), sliced
   thickly
500g pumpkin, peeled, chopped
   coarsely
3 teaspoons ground cumin
2 teaspoons ground coriander
1 cup (200g) couscous
1 cup (250ml) boiling water
20g butter
2 tablespoons coarsely chopped
   fresh flat-leaf parsley

serves 4
prep + cook time 40 minutes
per serving 9.8g fat; 1361kJ
(325 cal)

1 Preheat oven to 220°C/200°C
fan-forced.
2 Heat oil in medium flameproof
baking dish; cook garlic, onion and
pumpkin, stirring, until vegetables
are browned lightly. Add spices;
cook, stirring, about 2 minutes or
until fragrant.
3 Place baking dish in oven; roast
pumpkin mixture, uncovered, about
15 minutes or until pumpkin is just
tender.
4 Meanwhile, combine couscous
with the water and butter in large
heatproof bowl; cover, stand about
5 minutes or until liquid is absorbed,
fluffing with fork occasionally. Stir in
parsley.
5 Toss pumpkin mixture through
couscous.

pumpkin tagine with date couscous

2 tablespoons olive oil
1 large brown onion (200g),
   sliced thickly
3 cloves garlic, crushed
½ teaspoon ground chilli
½ teaspoon ground turmeric
1 teaspoon ground cinnamon
1 teaspoon ground coriander
1 teaspoon ground cumin
3 cups (750ml) vegetable stock
5 cups (800g) coarsely chopped
   pumpkin
1 cup (150g) frozen broad beans,
   thawed, peeled

1 tablespoon brown sugar
¾ cup (100g) coarsely chopped
   seeded dates
2 tablespoons coarsely chopped
   fresh coriander

date couscous
50g butter, chopped coarsely
2 cups (200g) couscous
2 cups (500ml) boiling water
½ cup (70g) coarsely chopped
   seeded dates
⅓ cup coarsely chopped fresh
   coriander

1 Heat oil in medium saucepan. Add onion, garlic and spices; cook, stirring, 3 minutes or until fragrant.
2 Add stock and pumpkin, bring to a boil; reduce heat, simmer, covered, about 10 minutes or until pumpkin is almost tender.
3 Uncover; simmer 5 minutes or until pumpkin mixture thickens slightly.
4 Meanwhile, make date couscous.
5 Add remaining ingredients to pumpkin mixture; cook, stirring, until heated through.
6 Serve pumpkin tagine with couscous.

date couscous Combine butter, couscous and the water in large heatproof bowl, cover; stand about 5 minutes or until liquid is absorbed, fluffing with fork occasionally. Stir in dates and coriander.

serves 4
prep + cook time 35 minutes
per serving 21.8g fat; 2861kJ (684)
tip You need to buy a piece of pumpkin weighing about 1kg to make this dish.

vegetable tagine with olive & parsley couscous

1 tablespoon olive oil
1 medium red onion (170g), sliced
  thinly
2 cloves garlic, crushed
1 teaspoon dried chilli flakes
1 teaspoon ground coriander
½ teaspoon ground turmeric
1 teaspoon cumin seeds
500g pumpkin, chopped coarsely
2 medium potatoes (400g), chopped
  coarsely

2½ cups (625ml) vegetable stock
300g can chickpeas, rinsed, drained
½ cup coarsely chopped fresh coriander

olive & parsley couscous
1½ cups (375ml) vegetable stock
1½ cups (300g) couscous
30g butter
1⅓ cups (200g) seeded kalamata olives
½ cup coarsely chopped fresh flat-leaf
  parsley

1 Heat oil in medium saucepan; cook onion, garlic and chilli, stirring, until onion softens. Add spices and seeds; cook, stirring, until mixture is fragrant. Add pumpkin and potato; stir to coat vegetables in spice mixture.
2 Stir in stock; bring to a boil. Reduce heat; simmer, uncovered, about 10 minutes or until vegetables are almost tender. Stir in chickpeas; simmer, uncovered, about 10 minutes or until vegetables are tender.
3 Meanwhile, make olive and parsley couscous.
4 Stir coriander into tagine. Serve couscous topped with vegetable tagine.

olive & parsley couscous Bring stock to a boil in medium saucepan. Remove from heat; stir in couscous and butter. Cover; stand about 5 minutes or until liquid is absorbed, fluffing with fork occasionally. Stir in olives and parsley.

serves 4
prep + cook time 40 minutes
per serving 14.4g fat; 2541kJ (607 cal)
tip You need a piece of pumpkin weighing approximately 600g for this recipe.

baked tomato couscous

serves 6
prep + cook time 45 minutes
per serving 5.9g fat; 882kJ (211 cal)
tip To make this a vegetarian couscous, replace the chicken stock with vegetable stock.

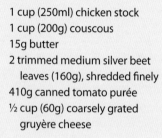

1 cup (250ml) chicken stock
1 cup (200g) couscous
15g butter
2 trimmed medium silver beet leaves (160g), shredded finely
410g canned tomato purée
½ cup (60g) coarsely grated gruyère cheese

1 Preheat oven to 200°C/180°C fan-forced. Oil shallow 1-litre (4-cup) ovenproof dish.
2 Bring stock to the boil in medium saucepan; remove from heat, add couscous and butter. Cover; stand about 5 minutes or until liquid is absorbed, fluffing with fork occasionally. Stir silver beet into couscous; season to taste.
3 Spoon couscous into dish; press down gently. Pour tomato over couscous, sprinkle with cheese.
4 Bake about 30 minutes or until cheese is browned lightly.

spiced cauliflower couscous

1 tablespoon olive oil
1 small brown onion (80g),
 sliced thinly
1 teaspoon ground coriander
½ small cauliflower (500g), cut into
 small florets
2 tablespoons water
⅓ cup coarsely chopped fresh
 coriander
1¼ cups (250g) couscous
1¼ cups (310ml) boiling water

serves 6
prep + cook time 25 minutes
per serving 3.4g fat; 844kJ (202 cal)

1 Heat oil in large saucepan, add onion; cook, stirring, until onion is soft. Add ground coriander and cauliflower; cook, stirring, until fragrant. Add the water; cook, covered, about 10 minutes or until cauliflower is tender and water absorbed. Stir in half the fresh coriander.
2 Meanwhile, combine couscous with the boiling water in large heatproof bowl, cover; stand about 5 minutes or until liquid is absorbed, fluffing with fork occasionally.
3 Stir cauliflower mixture into couscous; season to taste. Serve sprinkled with remaining fresh coriander.

spicy red couscous

··

1 tablespoon olive oil
1 tablespoon harissa
2 teaspoons sweet paprika
4 green onions, sliced thinly
1 cup (250ml) chicken stock
½ cup (125ml) water
1½ cups (300g) couscous
1 tablespoon lemon juice

1 Heat oil in medium saucepan, add harissa, paprika and half the onion; cook, stirring, about 2 minutes or until fragrant. Add stock and the water; bring to the boil. Remove from heat, add couscous; cover, stand about 5 minutes or until liquid is absorbed, fluffing with fork occasionally.
2 Stir juice into couscous; season to taste. Serve sprinkled with remaining onion.

··

serves 6
prep + cook time 15 minutes
per serving 3.6g fat; 928kJ (222 cal)

salads

orange & radish salad

4 medium oranges (960g)
500g red radishes, trimmed
1 tablespoon olive oil
2 teaspoons white wine vinegar
¼ cup finely chopped fresh mint

1 Finely grate 2 teaspoons rind from half an orange. Segment oranges over small bowl; reserve 1 tablespoon juice.
2 Using mandolin or V-slicer, slice radishes as thinly as possible.
3 Whisk reserved juice, oil and vinegar in medium bowl. Add rind, orange segments, radish and mint; toss gently. Serve immediately.

serves 4
prep + cook time 25 minute
per serving 5g fat; 535kJ (128 cal)
tip This recipe is best made just before serving; it will become soggy if left standing.

warm lamb tabbouleh

serves 4
prep + cook time 35 minutes
(+ refrigeration and standing time)
per serving 21.1g fat; 1852kJ
(443 cal)

500g lamb eye of loin, sliced thinly
2 cloves garlic, crushed
¼ cup (60ml) lemon juice
2 tablespoons olive oil
1 cup (160g) burghul
250g cherry tomatoes, halved
8 green onions, chopped thinly
¼ cup (60ml) lemon juice, extra
½ cup coarsely chopped fresh
    flat-leaf parsley
½ cup coarsely chopped fresh mint

1 Combine lamb, garlic, juice and half the oil in large bowl, cover; refrigerate 3 hours or overnight.
2 Cover burghul with cold water in small bowl; stand 15 minutes, drain. Rinse burghul under cold water; drain, squeeze out excess moisture.
3 Heat remaining oil in wok; stir-fry lamb mixture, in batches, until browned. Cover to keep warm.
4 Stir-fry burghul, tomato and onion in wok until onion is browned lightly.
5 Toss extra juice, parsley and mint through tabbouleh off the heat; serve with lamb mixture.

citrus chicken with chickpea salad

4 chicken breast fillets (800g),
  halved
1 tablespoon finely grated lemon
  rind
1 tablespoon finely grated lime rind
300g can chickpeas, rinsed, drained
1 medium red onion (170g),
  chopped finely
2 medium tomatoes (300g),
  chopped coarsely
1 tablespoon finely chopped fresh
  coriander leaves
1 medium avocado (250g), chopped
  coarsely
1 tablespoon lemon juice

serves 4
prep + cook time 40 minutes
(+ refrigeration time)
per serving 14.9g fat; 1480kJ
(353 cal)

1 Combine chicken and rinds in
medium bowl, cover; refrigerate
3 hours.
2 Combine chickpeas, onion,
tomato, coriander, avocado and juice
in medium bowl; mix well.
3 Cook chicken on heated oiled grill
plate (or grill or barbecue) until
chicken is browned both sides and
cooked through. Spoon chickpea
salad into serving bowls; top with
warm chicken.

merguez & couscous salad

··

500g merguez sausages
1½ cups (375ml) beef stock
1½ cups (300g) couscous
20g butter
1 tablespoon finely grated lemon rind
¾ cup coarsely chopped fresh flat-leaf parsley
120g baby rocket leaves
⅓ cup (50g) roasted pine nuts
2 fresh small red thai chillies, sliced thinly
1 small red onion (100g), sliced thinly
1 clove garlic, crushed
⅓ cup (80ml) lemon juice
2 tablespoons olive oil

1 Cook sausages on heated grill plate (or grill or barbecue) until browned and cooked through. Drain on absorbent paper; slice thickly.
2 Meanwhile, bring stock to a boil in medium saucepan. Remove from heat; stir in couscous and butter. Cover; stand about 10 minutes or until liquid is absorbed, fluffing with fork occasionally.
3 Place sausage and couscous in large bowl with remaining ingredients; toss gently to combine.

··

serves 4
prep + cook time 25 minutes
per serving 45g fat; 3621kJ (865 cal)

chicken, preserved lemon & green bean salad

serves 4
prep + cook time 20 minutes
per serving 20.2g fat; 1998kJ (477 cal)
tip You need to purchase a large barbecued chicken for this recipe.

1 cup (160g) sultanas
1 cup (250ml) warm water
¼ cup (60ml) lemon juice
1 barbecued chicken (900g)
175g baby green beans, trimmed
2 tablespoons finely chopped
   preserved lemon rind
340g jar marinated quartered
   artichokes, drained
2 cups firmly packed fresh flat-leaf
   parsley leaves
2 tablespoons olive oil
2 tablespoons white wine vinegar

1 Combine sultanas, the water and juice in medium bowl, cover; stand 5 minutes. Drain; discard liquid.
2 Meanwhile, discard skin and bones from chicken; slice meat thickly.
3 Boil, steam or microwave beans until tender; drain. Rinse under cold water; drain.
4 Place sultanas, chicken and beans in large bowl with remaining ingredients; toss gently to combine.

moroccan couscous
& chicken salad

1 cup (250ml) vegetable stock
1½ cups (300g) couscous
1 medium red onion (170g),
    sliced thinly
3 cups (480g) shredded barbecued
    chicken
½ cup (75g) coarsely chopped
    dried apricots
½ cup (80g) sultanas
¼ cup finely chopped fresh mint
1 tablespoon pine nuts
2 teaspoons cumin seeds
¾ cup (180ml) french dressing

serves 4
prep + cook time 15 minutes
per serving 10.5g fat; 2625kJ (628 cal)
tip You need to purchase a large
barbecued chicken for this recipe.

1 Bring stock to a boil in large
saucepan; remove from heat. Stir
in couscous. Cover; stand about
5 minutes or until stock is absorbed,
fluffing with fork occasionally. Stir
in onion, chicken, apricot, sultanas
and mint.
2 Meanwhile, dry-fry nuts and
seeds in small frying pan over low
heat until just fragrant. Add to
couscous with dressing; toss gently
to combine.

merguez, beetroot & lentil salad

....

2 cups (400g) brown lentils
2 sprigs fresh thyme
20 baby red beetroots (500g)
20 baby golden beetroots (500g)
8 merguez sausages (640g)
1 large brown onion (200g),
   chopped finely
2 teaspoons yellow mustard seeds
2 teaspoons ground cumin

1 teaspoon ground coriander
½ cup (125ml) chicken stock
300g spinach, trimmed, chopped coarsely

thyme dressing
1 teaspoon finely chopped fresh thyme
1 clove garlic, crushed
½ cup (125ml) red wine vinegar
¼ cup (60ml) extra virgin olive oil

1 Make thyme dressing.

2 Cook lentils with thyme sprigs, uncovered, in large saucepan of boiling water until tender; drain lentils, discard thyme sprigs. Place lentils in large bowl with half the dressing; toss gently to combine.

3 Meanwhile, discard leaves and most of the stalk from each beetroot. Boil, steam or microwave unpeeled beetroots until just tender; drain. When cool enough to handle, peel beetroots then cut in half.

4 Cook sausages in heated large oiled frying pan until browned and cooked through. Cool 5 minutes; slice thickly.

5 Reheat pan; cook onion, seeds, cumin and coriander, stirring, until onion softens. Add stock; bring to a boil. Remove from heat; stir in spinach.

6 Add spinach mixture, beetroot, sausage and remaining dressing to lentil mixture; toss gently to combine.

thyme dressing Combine ingredients in screw-top jar; shake well.

....

serves 4
prep + cook time 1 hour 20 minutes
per serving 45.2g fat; 3968kJ (948 cal)
tip When trimming the beetroots, leave a little of the stalk intact to prevent bleeding during cooking.

moroccan beef salad with couscous

serves 4
prep + cook time 30 minutes
per serving 14.2g fat; 2495kJ
(596 cal)

1 cup (250ml) vegetable stock
1½ cups (300g) couscous
500g beef rump steak
½ cup (75g) dried apricots, sliced
½ cup (80g) sultanas
1 medium red onion (170g), sliced
   thinly
¼ cup finely chopped fresh mint
2 tablespoons finely chopped
   fresh dill
1 tablespoon pine nuts
2 teaspoons cumin seeds
¾ cup (180ml) oil-free french
   dressing

1   Cook beef on heated oiled grill plate (or grill or barbecue) until browned both sides and cooked as desired. Cover, stand 5 minutes then slice thinly.

2   Meanwhile, bring stock to a boil in large pan, remove from heat; add couscous. Cover, stand about 5 minutes or until liquid is absorbed, fluffing with fork occasionally. Add apricots, sultanas, onion and herbs to couscous; mix gently.

3   Place pine nuts and cumin in dry small frying pan; stir over low heat until seeds are just fragrant and pine nuts are roasted. Combine seeds and nuts with dressing in small bowl; drizzle over beef and couscous.

grilled eggplant with tabbouleh

3 small tomatoes (270g)
¼ cup (40g) burghul
2 large eggplants (1kg)
⅓ cup (80ml) extra virgin olive oil
4 cups coarsely chopped fresh
    flat-leaf parsley
1 cup coarsely chopped fresh mint
1 medium red onion (170g),
    chopped finely
2 tablespoons lemon juice

serves 4
prep + cook time 25 minutes
(+ refrigeration time)
per serving 19.5g fat; 1225kJ
(293 cal)

1 Chop tomatoes finely, retaining as much juice as possible. Place tomato and juice on top of the burghul in small bowl; cover, refrigerate 2 hours or until burghul is soft.

2 Cut each eggplant into 8 wedges. Brush eggplant with half the oil; cook on heated grill plate (or grill or barbecue) about 10 minutes or until browned and tender.

3 Meanwhile, combine tomato mixture with the parsley, mint, onion, juice and remaining oil.

4 Serve tabbouleh with eggplant.

glossary

basil an aromatic herb; there are many types, but the most commonly used is sweet, or common, basil.

beans

broad also known as fava, windsor and horse beans; are available dried, fresh, canned and frozen. Fresh and frozen, they are best peeled twice (discarding both the outer long green pod and the beige-green tough inner shell).

cannellini small, dried white bean similar in appearance and flavour to great northern, navy or haricot bean.

beetroot also known as red beets; round root vegetable.

golden beetroot have a slightly sweeter flavour than the red variety.

blue-eye fillets also known as trevally, deep sea trevalla or blue-eye cod; thick, moist white-fleshed fish fillets.

burghul also known as bulghur wheat; hulled, steamed wheat kernels that, once dried, are crushed into various-sized grains.

butternut pumpkin used interchangeably with the word squash; is pear-shaped with orange skin and flesh.

capsicum also known as bell pepper or, simply, pepper. Discard seeds and membranes before use.

cardamom has an aromatic, sweetly rich flavour; available in pod, seed or ground form.

cayenne pepper an extremely hot, dried red chilli, usually purchased ground; both arbol and guajillo chillies are the fresh sources for cayenne.

cheese

fetta Greek in origin; a crumbly-textured goat or sheep-milk cheese with a sharp, salty taste.

parmesan also known as parmigiano; a hard, grainy cow-milk cheese.

chickpeas also called garbanzos, hummus or channa; an irregularly round sandy-coloured legume.

chilli use rubber gloves when seeding and chopping fresh chillies as they can burn your skin. Removing membranes and seeds lessens the heat level.

flakes, dried deep-red, dehydrated chilli slices and whole seeds.

red thai small, medium hot, and bright red in colour.

cinnamon dried inner bark of the shoots of the cinnamon tree; available in stick or ground form.

coriander also known as cilantro or chinese parsley; bright-green leafy herb with a pungent flavour. Also sold as seeds, whole or ground. The stems and roots of coriander are also used in Thai cooking. Coriander seeds are no substitute for fresh coriander.

cornflour also known as cornstarch; used as a thickening agent in cooking.

couscous a fine, grain-like cereal product, made from semolina.

cumin also known as zeera or comino; has a spicy, nutty flavour. Available in seed form or dried and ground.

currants, dried tiny, almost black, raisins.

dates fruit of the date palm tree, eaten fresh or dried. Oval, plump and thin-skinned, with a honey-sweet flavour and sticky texture.

eggplant also known as aubergine. Ranging in size from tiny to very large, and in colour from pale-green to deep-purple.

french-trimmed sometimes just seen as "frenched"; all excess sinew, gristle and fat from the bone end of meat cutlets, racks or shanks are removed and the bones scraped clean.

garam masala a blend of spices based on varying proportions of cardamom, cinnamon, cloves, coriander, fennel and cumin, roasted and ground together.

ginger

fresh also known as green or root ginger; a thick gnarled root of a tropical plant.

ground also known as powdered ginger; cannot be substituted for fresh ginger.

harissa a paste made from dried red chillies, garlic, oil and caraway seeds; is a staple of Moroccan cooking.

kalamata olives small, sharp-tasting, brine-cured black olives.

kumara Polynesian name of orange-fleshed sweet potato often confused with yam.

merguez a small, spicy sausage traditionally made with lamb and is easily identified by its chilli-red colour. Available from butchers, delicatessens and sausage specialty stores.

mince meat also known as ground meat, as in beef, pork, lamb, chicken and veal.

mustard seeds, yellow mild seeds, available from most major supermarkets and health food shops.

oil

mustard seed rich and full-bodied with a buttery, nutty flavour, but without the heat or strong mustard taste. It has a low saturated fat content and is high in omega-3 and monounsaturated fats.

olive made from ripened olives. Extra virgin and virgin are the best, while extra light or light refers to taste, not fat levels.

peanut pressed ground nuts; has a high smoke point (the capacity to handle high heat without burning).

vegetable any of a number of oils sourced from plants rather than animal fats.

onion

brown and white are interchangeable.

green also known as scallion, spring onion or, incorrectly, shallot; an immature onion having a long, bright-green edible stalk.

red also known as spanish, red spanish or bermuda onion; a sweet-flavoured, large, purple-red onion.

paprika ground dried red capsicum (bell pepper), available sweet or hot.

parsley, flat-leaf also known as continental parsley or italian parsley.

pine nut also known as pignoli; not in fact a nut but a small, cream-coloured kernel from pine cones.

pitta a wheat-flour pocket bread also known as lebanese bread. Is sold in large, flat pieces that separate into two thin rounds or small thick pieces called pocket pitta.

polenta also known as cornmeal; a flour-like cereal made of dried corn (maize). Also the name of the dish made from it.

preserved lemon lemons bottled in salt and oil for several months. Rinse the lemons well then remove and discard flesh, using the rind only.

prawns also called shrimp.

radish a peppery vegetable related to the mustard plant. The small round red variety is the mildest.

ras el hanout a classic spice blend used in Moroccan cooking. The name means "top of the shop" and it is the very best spice blend that a spice merchant has to offer. The blends may often contain more than 20 different spices.

rocket also known as arugula, rugula and rucola; a peppery-tasting green leaf. Baby rocket leaves are both smaller and less peppery.

saffron available in strands or ground form; imparts a yellow-orange colour to food once infused.

silver beet also known as swiss chard; a member of the beet family grown for its tasty green leaves and celery-like stems.

spinach also known as english spinach and, incorrectly, silver beet.

sultanas dried grapes also known as golden raisins.

tomatoes

cherry small, round tomatoes also known as tiny tim or tom thumb.

yellow teardrop small yellow pear-shaped tomatoes.

turmeric a rhizome related to galangal and ginger; must be grated or pounded to release its somewhat acrid aroma and pungent flavour.

vinegar

balsamic originally from Modena, Italy, there are now many balsamic vinegars on the market ranging in pungency and quality depending on how long they have been aged; use the most expensive sparingly.

red wine based on fermented red wine.

white wine made from white wine.

zucchini also known as courgette.

conversion charts

MEASURES

One Australian metric measuring cup holds approximately 250ml, one Australian metric tablespoon holds 20ml, one Australian metric teaspoon holds 5ml.

The difference between one country's measuring cups and another's is within a 2- or 3-teaspoon variance, and will not affect your cooking results. North America, New Zealand and the United Kingdom use a 15ml tablespoon. All cup and spoon measurements are level. The most accurate way of measuring dry ingredients is to weigh them. When measuring liquids, use a clear glass or plastic jug with metric markings.

We use large eggs with an average weight of 60g.

WARNING This book may contain recipes for dishes made with raw or lightly cooked eggs. These should be avoided by vulnerable people such as pregnant and nursing mothers, invalids, the elderly, babies and young children.

DRY MEASURES

METRIC	IMPERIAL
15g	½oz
30g	1oz
60g	2oz
90g	3oz
125g	4oz (¼lb)
155g	5oz
185g	6oz
220g	7oz
250g	8oz (½lb)
280g	9oz
315g	10oz
345g	11oz
375g	12oz (¾lb)
410g	13oz
440g	14oz
470g	15oz
500g	16oz (1lb)
750g	24oz (1½lb)
1kg	32oz (2lb)

LIQUID MEASURES

METRIC	IMPERIAL
30ml	1 fl oz
60ml	2 fl oz
100ml	3 fl oz
125ml	4 fl oz
150ml	5 fl oz (¼ pint/1 gill)
190ml	6 fl oz
250ml	8 fl oz
300ml	10 fl oz (½ pint)
500ml	16 fl oz
600ml	20 fl oz (1 pint)
1000ml (1 litre)	1¾ pints

LENGTH MEASURES

METRIC	IMPERIAL
3mm	⅛in
6mm	¼in
1cm	½in
2cm	¾in
2.5cm	1in
5cm	2in
6cm	2½in
8cm	3in
10cm	4in
13cm	5in
15cm	6in
18cm	7in
20cm	8in
23cm	9in
25cm	10in
28cm	11in
30cm	12in (1ft)

OVEN TEMPERATURES

These oven temperatures are only a guide for conventional ovens.
For fan-assisted ovens, check the manufacturer's manual.

	°C (CELSIUS)	°F (FAHRENHEIT)	GAS MARK
Very low	120	250	½
Low	150	275–300	1–2
Moderately low	160	325	3
Moderate	180	350–375	4–5
Moderately hot	200	400	6
Hot	220	425–450	7–8
Very hot	240	475	9

index

Published in 2011 by Octopus
Publishing Group Limited based
on materials licensed to it by
ACP Magazines Ltd, a division of
PBL Media Pty Limited
54 Park St, Sydney
GPO Box 4088, Sydney, NSW 2001
phone (02) 9282 8618;
fax (02) 9267 9438
acpbooks@acpmagazines.com.au;
www.acpbooks.com.au

OCTOPUS BOOKS
Design: Chris Bell
Food Director: Pamela Clark

Published and Distributed in the
United Kingdom by Octopus Publishing
Group Limited
Endeavour House
189 Shaftesbury Avenue
London WC2H 8JY
United Kingdom
phone + 44 (0) 207 632 5400;
fax + 44 (0) 207 632 5405
aww@octopusbooks.co.uk;
www.octopusbooks.co.uk
www.australian-womens-weekly.com

Printed and bound in China

International foreign language rights,
Brian Cearnes, ACP Books
bcearnes@acpmagazines.com.au

To order books:
telephone LBS on 01903 828 503
order online at
www.australian-womens-weekly.com
or www.octopusbooks.co.uk